Michèle-Caroline Heck

THE GOLDEN BOOK OF
COLMAR
AND THE ROUTE DU VIN

BONECHI

CONTENTS

© Copyright by CASA EDITRICE BONECHI
Via Cairoli 18b - 50131 Firenze, Italia
Tel. +39 055576841 - Fax +39 0555000766 - E-mail: bonechi@bonechi.it - Internet: www.bonechi.it

Printed in Italy by Centro Stampa Editoriale Bonechi.

Translated by Studio Comunicare, Florence.

Photographs from the Archives of Casa Editrice Bonechi, taken by Luigi Di Giovine.
Photographs by Andrea Pistolesi: pages 8, 14 below, 30, 38-39, 40 below, 44, 45 below, 46 below, 48 below, 55 above, 57, 58, 60-63.
Photographs by J. P. T.: pages 52 above, 53 centre and below.
Photographs kindly provided by Jardin des papillons exotiques vivants, Hunawihr: page 53 above.

ISBN 88-8029-006-1

* * *

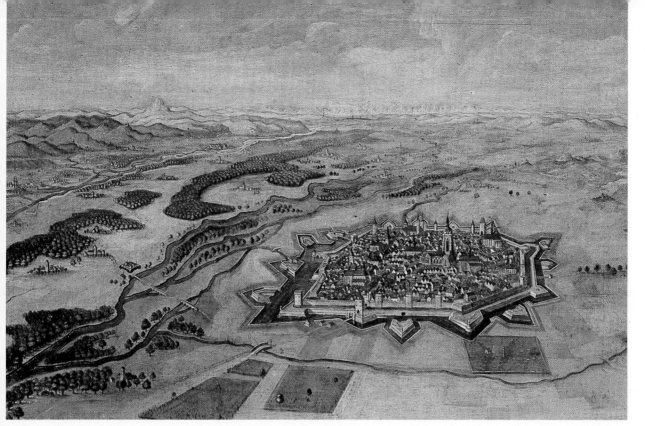

Colmar in the 17th century

COLMAR

Situated in the Alsatian plain near the foothills of the Vosges, and more or less equidistant from Strasbourg and Basle, Colmar at the beginning of the 17th century appeared to be a town well integrated into a favourable site, as can be seen from the painting reproduced on the previous page. To the West the lower slopes of the Vosges, covered in thick forests, still hide a number of the forts which were so numerous in the Middle Ages. To the East the rivers Ill and Thur divide into a number of winding tributaries and the forests of the Ried unfold between these waterways and the Rhine, beyond which, not far off, rise the hills of the Black Forest.

Although archeological research has furnished abundant evidence for Man's presence in the region since the Neolithic period, and the Bronze and Iron Ages have left behind some exceptional remains, Colmar does not make its appearance on the historical scene until much later. The important remains of the Gallo-Roman civilisation, to be found today in the Unterlinden Museum, provide evidence for occupation of the countryside or at least of the Horburg site.

It was in the 9th century that Colmar, known at that time as Columbaria, was first mentioned in a document. The present town was then just a vast estate, a residence which was used on several occasions by the Carolingian Kings. It is between the 10th century (a period in which the Royal Estate was divided into two major parts, one going to the Chapter of Constance, the other to the Swiss Abbey of Payerne) and the beginning of the 13th that one can situate the first important period of growth of what was up to then only a large village...

In fact the 13th century constitutes an essential stage of development in its history. Colmar was raised to the status of a municipality before coming directly under Imperial rule. This political development was accompanied by the first mention of the townsfolk, the new fortifications, and the presence of the Imperial Eagle on the town's seal. In 1278 Rodolphe of Hapsburg granted the town a municipal constitution whose statutes gave it a certain political autonomy: the area of competence of the provost and council were fixed, the townsfolk coming directly under the protection of the Empire. The end of the Middle Ages was marked by conflicts through which the bourgeoisie confirmed its new power; there were struggles with the nobles whose role had been limited by the new constitution of 1360, there were struggles in the context of the great confrontations of the period, there was the struggle within the Decapole, that well known association of the ten imperial towns of Alsace.

However in spite of the tensions Colmar became at this time a great artistic centre. Around the Collegiate church of St. Martin, whose construction was started soon after 1235, there grew up the establishments of the Orders of the Mendicant Friars, of the Dominicans, of the Franciscans, all very active in the Rhine Valley from the 13th century onwards. This ferment in religious life which can be connected with the development of Rhenish mysticism is reflected in the artistic production of the period. If the 13th and 14th centuries have left us important works of architecture and sculpture, the development of easel painting as well as the large number of panel paintings of the «Late Gothic» period prove that there must have been many studios flourishing in Colmar during the 15th and early 16th centuries. Martin Schongauer painted among other things the well known «Virgin of the Rose Bush» and his name became known in Europe at the same time as his copper engravings, which are exceptional for their freedom of expression. His reputation reached well beyond the frontiers of Alsace. Dürer himself visited the Colmar master's studio after his death.

Like Renaissance Art the Protestant Reformation was late in coming to Colmar. The first protestant service was held in the former Franciscan church on 15th May 1575 and the new religion rapidly assumed an important place in the city. However the situation was unstable and the 16th and 17th centuries were a time of crisis for the town in spite of its economic dynamism. After many vicissitudes the final outcome of the Thirty Years' War saw the integration of Colmar into the possessions of the French monarchy. Firstly as a consequence of the Treaty of Rueil in 1635, but above all after its military annexation by Louis XIV's troops in 1673 and the Treaty of Nijmegen in 1678, Colmar became a French royal town. The arrival in 1698 of the Jesuits of Ensisheim, who installed themselves in St. Peter's Priory (replaced during the following century by a whole complex of buildings), demonstrated the royal wish to give the Catholic Church a primary role in the education and religious life of the town again. It was in the same year that the Sovereign Council of Alsace established itself in Colmar. This institution had an importance to which both its building, reconstructed round about 1770, and the eminent jurists who were members of it, bear witness. The latter constituted a cultural élite in frequenting which, Voltaire, who was in Colmar during 1753-54, found consolation for his misfortunes. After the French Revolution with all its consequences, Colmar became the seat both of a Prefect and of a Court of Appeal and thus integrated itself even further into the French administration. Its agricultural and commercial roles continued to provide the impetus for a town which the industrial revolution had hardly touched. Naturally urban development during the period of German annexation from 1870 to 1918 changed the appearance of some streets and squares but it must be stated that the contemporary development of Colmar occurred smoothly without any sudden break with its past. This period is still connected with the name of Bartholdi and the museum which Colmar has devoted to his work, which has recently been completely modernized, presents important aspects of the town's history as well as essential elements of the life and work of this sculptor whose most famous creation is the Statue of Liberty.

The changes occurring during the 19th century together with the ravages of two world wars did not, fortunately, deprive Colmar of the remains of its historical heritage. It is with this heritage that Colmar has witnessed since 1945 an unprecedented growth taking its population to nearly 70,000 inhabitants, together with the development of an industrial activity which, without undue stress, has complemented and not damaged the town's other resources. Tourists are not mistaken when they come in ever larger numbers, attracted by its gastronomic reputation and the wines from the nearby vineyards, by the development of its architectural heritage of which the restoration of the rue des Tanneurs is only the most striking example, and by the Unterlinden Museum of which the Issenheim Altar-piece is the jewel.

Place de l'Ancienne Douane. The Koïfhus

THE KOÏFHUS

This complex of buildings was the very heart of the economic and political life of Colmar during the Middle Ages. The first floor of the main building of the Koïfhus or old Customs House was occupied by the town administration while the ground floor was a goods warehouse for storing imported goods on which duty was to be levied. It was surrounded by other buildings now long gone, the Grande Boucherie (the Abattoir or Slaughterhouse), the Eisenhaus or depository for iron and other met-als, the Ankenhaus for fats, the monetary workshop, the Corn Exchange and the Salt Exchange.

The oldest building in the Koïfhus complex, built in yellow sandstone from Rouffach, was finished in 1480 as is indicated by an inscription held by an angel: ANNO MCCCCLXXX ward dies huss gemachet. It is a vast two-storied rectangular building with a steeply pitched roof. Decoration is limited to the openings: a large doorway surmounted by a canopy with the double-headed eagle, the symbol of the Holy Roman Empire, beside which there is a smaller lateral door with an ogee lintel bearing the arms of the city of Colmar, a falling star. One finds the same arrangement on the north side, which allows vehicles loaded with merchandise to cross the hall to unload it. The windows are characteristically Gothic — rectangular with moulded mullions. In the bevelled corners of the building a half-length statue of a soldier holds a shield bearing the city arms. The interior of the edifice is very sobre, wooden ceilings being supported by stone pillars. On the first floor the stained-glass windows depict the coats of arms of the towns belonging to the Decapole (Haguenau, Colmar,

Sélestat, Wissembourg, Landau, Obernai, Rosheim, Kaysersberg, Munster, Turckheim, Mulhouse); this, in fact, was the room where the representatives of these towns held their meetings.

To this, the main part as well as the oldest part of the complex, is joined a smaller building. This has an arcaded ground floor with above it a loggia giving on to the Place de l'Ancienne Douane and having a polygonal turret, with a very richly decorated door, housing a staircase. On the west side, access to the rooms is via a double flight of stairs with stone banisters covered over with a roof whose wooden ceiling has recently been restored. In front of the building there is a stone column erected in 1543 to commemorate the victory of the Emperor Charles V over the Duke of Clèves.

The complex is completed by a third building whose ornamentation is characteristically Renaissance: semi-circular archways on the ground floor, fluted pillars of which two are decorated with masks on the first floor, and above all the monumental gable with its curves and counter-curves. It was constructed at the end of the 16th century as a market for butter and imported fats.

THE PLACE DE L'ANCIENNE DOUANE

This square was created only after the mill canal which formerly crossed it was covered over and the Grande Boucherie (the Slaughterhouse) and the 13th century mill which used to stand there had been demolished. In 1897 a stone fountain was erected having an eight-sided basin and a tall central pillar on which is a bronze statue by Auguste Bartholdi of Baron Lazare of Schwendi, the lord of Holandsberg (1522-1583).

THE PLACE DU MARCHE AUX FRUITS

This square is also a recent innovation being created only at the time of the French Revolution when the Kornhaus or Corn Exchange which used to stand there was demolished. Apart from the Koïfhus on the north side there are two other important buildings in the square. There is Kern House on the south side, a tall building dating from the end of the 16th or the beginning of the 17th century, which unites in the same façade Gothic mullion windows and a characteristic Alsatian Renaissance roof. The Courthouse on the east side occupies the former Sovereign Council building. Built by the Colmar architects Chassain and Blaise de Rungs in 1769-1771, it is in the French Classical style. It replaced an older building, the Wagkeller, the former meeting place of the nobles and then from 1459 until the installation of the Sovereign Council in Colmar in 1698, the town hall.

*Place de la Cathédrale,
Adolph's house*

The Koïfhus, southern façade

The Koïfhus, western façade

*Place de l'Ancienne Douane.
The Schwendi fountain*

THE RUE DES MARCHANDS

It was only in 1783 that the Schädelgasse, Skull Street, changed its name to rue des Marchands. A group of houses facing the Koïfhus are of particular interest, they formerly constituted the Salzkasten, the Salt Exchange. There are numerous houses in this street which have the characteristic architecture of 16th century Colmar. The ground floors are stone with moulded doorways, sometimes arched, while the upper floors are half-timbered, often overhanging. The great age of these houses is attested to by the dates which are engraved on the lintels of the doors or on the keystones of the arches. Some are still decorated with old painted signs.

The house at no. 23, apart from the quality of its architecture, is noteworthy for the inscription which is set into the facade: it is in fact a banishment stone dated 1358. This reminds us of the troubles which shook Colmar during the 14th century, the building having been ordered to be razed to the ground by Prince Rodolphe, Duke of Austria and Governor of Alsace.

The house at no. 52 takes its name, 'The Bear', from the sculpted figure of a bear which used to be on the corner. The house at no. 42 is interesting because it is still laid out in the form of a 16th century artisan's atelier or workshop. The three story house at no. 38b, which was constructed on the site of an older building, with its very regular design and its decoration of moulded grotesque masks, is a fine example of the 18th century architecture of Colmar.

On the same side no. 34, «Zum grienen Hus», the Green House, is one of the oldest, being dated 1435. It was here that the Colmar painter Gaspard Isenmann, who painted the panels of the main altar at the collegiate church of St.

Martin from 1462 to 1465, now at the Unterlinden Museum, used to live. No. 36, the Rose House, was the home of the Mercers' Guild until 1521.

The house at no. 9 is interesting firstly for its design: a stonework ground floor with two half-timbered floors above, the third floor being set back and opening onto the exterior via a loggia. The decoration is concentrated on the wooden frames of the windows which are flanked by small columns of carved wood. This decoration is also exhibited by the balustrade on the third floor as well as by the columns supporting the eaves, one of which bears the date 1588. In the corner niche on the first floor there is a wooden statue of a draper holding a tape measure, which dates from 1609 and which came from another house in the rue Berthe Molly.

The house at no. 30, now the Bartholdi Museum, is the birth place of the Colmar sculptor Auguste Bartholdi. It is an 18th century town house, largely rebuilt in the 19th century but still retaining many elements of its original style.

The house «Zum Swan», 'The Swan', is typically Gothic in style. On the ground floor the two doors are ogee arched with finial decoration. On the first floor a very beautiful oriel window occupies the centre of the façade, the two windows being ogee arched with blind trefoil tracery on both sides, while the statues which formerly stood in the two corner niches are now missing. The lower part of the oriel is occupied by a panel decorated with blind tracery.

The house «zum Swan» in the Rue Schongauer

No. 9 Rue des Marchands

Pfister house, detail

Pfister house, detail

Pfister house

PFISTER HOUSE

This house was built in 1537 by the toque merchant Ludwig Scherer on the site of an older house. By 1567 it belonged to a draper, Claus Stattmann, to whom we are endebted for the external mural decoration. In 1596 it belonged to yet another merchant who had it restored in 1613. The name it now bears is that of the 19th century proprietors.

It is a vast three story house in Rouffach limestone with a very fine oriel window on the corner. The ground floor with its great arches served from the very beginning as a shop. In the upper stories the mullion windows are still in the Gothic tradition. The wooden gallery on the second floor is supported by stone consoles. The upper floors are reached by a spiral staircase in the octagonal turret. However this building is particularly noteworthy for its mural decoration. The iconography is characteristic of humanist taste of the period associating as it does biblical themes (the four Evangelists, the Fathers of the Church, in the bottom row; scenes from Genesis in the second row; and other scenes from the Old Testament in the third row) with allegorical figures (Love, Faith, Justice, Hope, Force and Temperance in the third row) and effigies of Emperors (Maximilian, Charles, Ferdinand under the second floor gallery). The house was restored in 1971.

PLACE DE LA CATHEDRALE

The square was created in 1784 on the site of the former St. Martin's cemetery. There are two buildings worthy of note. Firstly, Adolphe House, named after the 19th century owner who uncovered the Gothic windows. The oldest parts of the house date from the 14th century, thus the tracery of the great second floor window is very similar to that of the choir windows in the nearby collegiate church. However the building underwent alterations in the 16th century as is shown by the date, 1584, on the door in the lateral façade. The upper part with its half-timbering is similarly a later addition.

THE OLD GUARD HOUSE

This building which bears the architect's initials, A.M., on one of the keystones of the loggia was constructed in 1575 on the site of St. James' Chapel which had been the chapel of St. Martin's cemetery since the 13th century. The decoration, which is of very fine quality, is concentrated on the main entrance, which is semicircular, and on the loggia. The richness in the ornamentation is shown by the use of fluted columns supporting an entablature, and by the decorative motifs such as the muzzles of lions, masks, and iron-work motifs arranged as a frieze on the loggia. This building is considered to be among the most beautiful remaining from the second half of the 16th century in Alsace.

Place de la Cathédrale,
Adolph's house

The Old Guard House

The Collegiate Church of St. Martin,
south façade

THE COLLEGIATE CHURCH OF ST. MARTIN

St. Martin's church in Colmar is one of the most beautiful examples of Gothic architecture still extant in the Haut-Rhin. Its great size is undoubtedly the reason it is often wrongly described as a «cathedral». Unlike Strasbourg or Basle Colmar has never been a bishop's seat and St. Martin's was initially just a simple parish church.

Recent excavations, however, have revealed that from the 11th century there existed a church with a square choir and a projecting transept to which was added later the solid mass on the west side. It was only in 1235 that St. Martin's became a collegiate church and the installation of this college of canons (secular monks) marked the beginning of a phase of massive reconstruction.

The work on the new church, which was in the Gothic style, started on the eastern side with the construction of the transept between 1240 and 1260 or thereabouts. The tympanum above the doorway in the south façade shows, arranged concentrically, a Last Judgement above the legend of St. Nicholas. The nave which was finished about 1270, testifies, by its refusal to imitate Strasbourg Cathedral which must have been *the* model at the time, to the great variety of Gothic forms existing in Alsace. At Colmar, for example, there is a significant amount of bare wall separating the arcades of the upper windows. Similarly the many shafted piers have been replaced by circular piers flanked by four small columns, which has the effect of underlining the massiveness of the support. The west face, which was finished much later, was intended to have a harmonious façade with two towers but only the south tower was ever finished. It was finished in the

middle of the 14th century. The tympanum of the west door, which was done a little after 1300, shows an Adoration of the Magi and a Christ in Judgement.

The second important phase of the Gothic rebuilding was the reconstruction of the Choir. This was probably conceived by Master William of Marburg before 1350 and was carried out before 1360, although it was only much later that the vaulting in certain parts was finished. The plan of the choir is somewhat unusual. It is surrounded by a series of intercommunicating chapels which are situated between the buttresses. Together with the doorways, the sculpted consoles illustrating the Passion of Christ which decorate the upper parts of the walls, constitute the major part of the older decoration of the building.

The stained-glass windows date mainly from the beginning of the 20th century with the exception of three beautiful scenes from the Old Testament and the Passion which come from the church of the Dominicans, but which are at present in the north bay of the narthex of St. Martin's.

The Collegiate Church of St. Martin, the interior.

The Collegiate Church of St. Martin, detail of the sculptured decoration.

Dominican Church.

On the following pages:

The interior of the Dominican Church.

Dominican Church, Martin Schongauer, The Virgin of the Rosery.

THE CHURCH OF THE DOMINICANS

From the 13th century onwards the Mendicant Orders were extremely active in Alsace, and the Dominicans and Franciscans in particular built a large number of churches. Colmar did not escape this trend which was marked by the foundation of the churches of the Dominicans, of the Dominican Nuns of Unterlinden and of St. Catherine, and of the Franciscans. The Dominican ideals of poverty and austerity are reflected in the structure of their church. The very long ambulatory is supported by simple buttresses rather than flying buttresses. The bell tower is reduced to its simplest possible form. The most astonishing feature is the way the space inside the church is exploited. The use of tall columns into which the great arcades penetrate directly without the use of intervening capitals breaks up the space very little giving an impression of unity and great size which is reinforced by the very small difference in height between the central nave and the side aisles which have a wooden ceiling. The choir on the other hand is vaulted with pointed arches. The construction of this church must undoubtedly be placed at the beginning of the 14th century.

One of the great riches of this church is the large number of stained-glass windows dating mainly from the 14th century. However one can also see there, on temporary exhibition, the Virgin of the Rose Bush, Martin Schongauer's masterpiece painted in 1473 for the Collegiate Church of St. Martin.

Martin Schongauer, who was almost certainly born in Colmar round about 1450 and whose father came from Augsburg, left a highly original corpus of work both in the field of copper engraving and in that of painting. The Virgin of the Rose Bush shows the Virgin and Child seated on a lawn with rose bushes in the background and, perched on the rose bushes, birds. Two angels hovering above hold the Virgin's crown. Here Schongauer is taking up the theme of the Virgin in the garden but he manages to combine a monumental force with the tenderness of the subject. This is accentuated by the intensity of the plastic values of all the elements in the composition, thus creating one of the great masterpieces of North European painting in the late Middle Ages.

THE MAISON DES TETES

It was this house, constructed in 1609 for the Colmar merchant Anton Burger, whose dates and arms can be seen at the top of the gable, which gave its name in 1888 to the street in which it stands. The style of the façade, the mullion windows, the tall fluted gable, are all features very similar to those of other buildings of the same period in Colmar, for example, the Maison Kern in the Place du Marché-aux-fruits. However what distinguishes this building is the profusion of decorative elements — caryatides, heads, and grimacing masks — which moreover are not simply limited to the frames of the doorway and the oriel but are also to be found on the jambs and mullions of the windows. It does not appear, however, that the overall scheme is the result of any coherent iconographic plan. On top of the gable there is a statue representing an Alsatian cooper. It dates from 1902 and is the work of Auguste Bartholdi.

The Maison des Têtes

18

THE CONVENT OF THE DOMINICAN NUNS OF UNTERLINDEN

This convent was founded at the beginning of the 13th century by two aristocratic widows from Colmar, Agnès de Mittelnheim and Agnès de Hergheim. In 1252 the nuns established themselves for good in the place known as Sub Tillia (underneath the lime trees or Unter den Linden). The convent soon assumed considerable importance both material and spiritual.

In 1269 the choir of the church was consecrated by Albert the Great, Bishop of Ratisbonne. In 1289 the cloisters were finished. The convent was an important centre of Rhenish mysticism. Master Eckhart stayed there in 1322 while Tauler of Strasbourg made frequent visits. The wealth and fame of the Unterlinden nuns continued to increase up until the 15th century. The 16th century however saw the beginning of the decline of the convent. In the 18th century the convent must have taken on a new lease of life, since there are alterations to the buildings dating from this period. An extra storey was added to the cloisters and the nave of the chapel was modified. In 1792 the sisters finally left the convent.

The building was saved from demolition in 1849 by Louis Hugot who two years before had created the Société Schongauer. In fact by installing the Roman mosaic from Bergheim in the former convent and by moving a collection of old paintings, confiscated at the time of the French Revolution, there in 1892 the Société Schongauer laid the basis for the Museum whose development it continues to promote with the help of the town even today.

Unterlinden Museum (former Dominican Convent)

THE UNTERLINDEN MUSEUM

The Medieval architecture of the Dominican Convent of Unterlinden constitutes a site of exceptional quality for the museum's collections which have not stopped growing since 1849. However although the most famous of its works, such as the panel paintings of Martin Schongauer and the Colmar School, the Issenheim altar-piece by Grünewald and the Romanesque and Gothic sculptures, blend in particularly well with this medieval building it should not be forgotten that in addition to these masterpieces the Unterlinden Museum also attempts to put on display a much wider view of the history of art and of civilisation.

The Archeological Section allows us to follow technical development from the polished stone tools of the Neolithic Period to the jewelry of the Bronze and Iron Ages. The Gallo-Roman Period is richly documented for living conditions and all aspects of daily life, by the floor mosaic from Bergheim, as well as for religious beliefs and practices, for which evidence is provided by funerary stones and the statues of Roman and Gaulish divinities.

The quality of the bronze fibulae of the Merovingian Period blends smoothly into the following period. However the Middle Ages is represented mainly by a series of Romanesque sculptures including several consoles from the former church at Alspach. The Gothic Period is well represented by sculptures from the 13th, 14th and particularly the 15th centuries, by a large number of painted panels, from the anonymous painters of the beginning of the 15th century to Gaspard Isenmann and Schongauer, as well as by the minor arts among which should be noted a very rare Alsatian tapestry on the theme of the Fountain of Youth.

The Modern Period from the Renaissance to the beginning of the 20th century testifies to the existence of a brilliant civilisation which was able to develop handicrafts and technics in the service of a style of life, sometimes luxurious, which found its expression in furniture, the decorative arts, ironwork, weapons, pewter, porcelaine and vast stoves. Precise military and historical memories, the testimonies of the often violent movements of history, can be contrasted with the popular arts and traditions. These illustrate the way in which local customs are rooted in such things as painted furniture, costume, household utensils, the tools of the wine-maker, the winepress and the wine-cellar with its decorated barrels.

Wine-grower's cellar, old presses

The cloister

Wine-grower's cellar, barrels

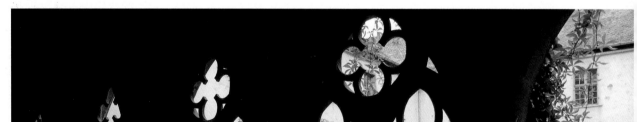

The chapel   *Grünewald's Issenheim altar-piece: the Angels' Concert and the Nativity*

However this evocation of a relatively recent period as well as that
of the romantic Alsace of castles
and ruined abbeys does not
exhaust the list. Over the last
twenty years or more the Unterlinden Museum has opened its
doors to contemporary art and the
presence of works by Renoir,
Monet, Rouault, Picasso, Braque,
Léger and Poliakoff to cite only a
few, demonstrates how it has succeeded in uniting the present century to its older inheritance.

THE ISSENHEIM ALTAR-PIECE

The Antonine Order has a special
place in the religious history of the
Middle Ages, and the continuously
renewed privileges accorded it by
the Popes are proof of the high
reputation which its medical activities justly earned it. The convent founded by the Antonine
Order at Issenheim near Guebwiller to the south of Colmar is no
exception to this rule. The altar-
piece of the Annunciation, painted
by Martin Schongauer for this institution while Jean d'Orlier
(1460-1490) was preceptor, is a
prime example of the riches which
these monks had in their possession.
However this work seems a trifle
by comparison with the majestic
ensemble of sculpture and painting
which constitutes the new major
altar-piece for the monastery's
chapel and which is usually simply
called the Issenheim Altar-Piece. It
consists on the one hand of a

23

series of wooden sculptures executed at the end of the 15th century by the artist Nicolas de Haguenau during the preceptorship of Jean d'Orlier and on the other hand of a series of painted panels, either fixed or pivoting like shutters in front of the sculptures, the work of a master who has been much studied and yet of whom we still know little, to whom the name of Grünewald is most correctly given. These paintings were executed during the preceptorship of Jean d'Orlier's successor, Guido Guersi (1490-1516), and probably from 1512-1516.

The precious and exceptional nature of this artistic ensemble does not allow this transformable altarpiece to be exhibited as originally intended. The Unterlinden Museum, in whose possession it is, has found it necessary to exhibit the different panels separately in order to avoid constant handling, which would be extremely deleterious to its good conservation. After seeing the tragic interpretation of the Crucifixion, which is flanked by the monumental figures of St. Sebastian on the left and of St. Anthony on the right, and which is placed above a predella showing the Entombment, the visitor is forced to use his imagination in order to reconstitute the sight which the opening of the first set of shutters would have revealed. This would have consisted of Grünewald's rendering of, in sequence, the Annunciation, the concert of Angels, the Nativity and the Resurrection which are now exhibited separately. The opening of the second set of shutters revealed to view the other two painted panels, the Temptation of St. Anthony and the Visit of St. Anthony to St. Paul, which flanked the central group of sculptures: St.

The Issenheim altar-piece: the Temptation of St. Anthony and the Meeting of St. Anthony and St. Paul in the desert

The Issenheim altar-piece: St. Sebastian, Crucifixion, St. Anthony and the Entombment

The Issenheim altar-piece: sculptured part, St. Augustin, St. Anthony and St. Jerome, Christ and the twelve Apostles

Martin Schongauer's Orlier altar-piece of the Annunciation.

Augustin, St. Anthony and St. Jerome above the Christ and the Apostles of the predella. This ensemble remains one of the great masterpieces of the entire history of painting.

THE MIDDLE AGES AND THE RENAISSANCE

The art of these two periods, at whose junction the Issenheim Altar-piece is situated, constitutes the bulk of the Unterlinden Museum's collections. In sculpture there is a steady movement from the bas-reliefs of the Romanesque period to the Gothic sculpture-in-the-round of the 13th and 14th centuries, such as the monumental statues from St. Martin's church, while the 15th century saw the growth of sculpture in wood, which favoured the search for an intense expressivity before works such as the altar-piece in limestone from Champagne dated 1522 signaled the arrival in the region of Renaissance forms.

Paintings, from a very rich Crucifixion dated about 1400 to the large altarpiece of the Passion, painted in the period 1462-1465 by Gaspard Isenmann for the Collegiate Church of St. Martin, show the continued attachment of Alsatian and Rhenish artists to the tradition of the gilded background. Martin Schongauer renewed pictorial forms by combining the precision and certainty of line, as shown by his engravings, with the force of plastic expression.

The so-called minor arts complete our knowledge of the artistic creativity of the period, work in precious metals, bronze, ivory and tapestry. For example, the tapestry which represents men and women issuing rejuvenated from the Fountain of Youth shows us a rich princely or bourgeois society seeking by every means, symbolically or in dream at least, to escape from death which was all too close and familiar.

Gaspard Isenmann, Pietà and Entombment

Passion altar-piece

THE PLACE RAPP

The Boulevard du Champ de Mars which forms the eastern side of this square runs along the original city wall dating from 1220. In the centre of the square, which has been turned into a car park, there stands the monument to General Rapp, the work of Bartholdi executed in 1855. The statue, which shows him standing, rests on a granite plinth on which are engraved his feats of arms and the words which he pronounced at the seige of Danzig «Ma parole est sacrée» («My word is sacred»). General Jean Rapp was born in Colmar, in the Koïfhus, on the 27th November 1771. He rose rapidly from the rank of private to that of general in the Napoleonic army, and distinguished himself by his great courage at the Battle of Austerlitz and in the defence of Dantzig. He died at Rheinweiler on the 8th November 1826.

Place Rapp, the statue of General Rapp

THE CHAMP DE MARS

The lay-out of the Public Gardens was conceived by Prefect Félix Desportes in 1804. At the centre of the garden, where all the alleys converge, stands a monumental fountain dedicated to Admiral Bruat which was inaugurated in 1864 and which is yet again the work of Bartholdi. Admiral Armand Joseph Bruat was born in Colmar on 27th May 1796 and died there in November 1855 following his return from the Crimean War during which he was the Commander-in-Chief of the French Fleet. Of Bartholdi's original work only the Admiral's statue remains. The circular pink limestone basin of the fountain, decorated with four figures representing America, Africa, Asia and Oceania, was destroyed in 1940 and replaced in 1958 by the present basin, the work of the Parisian sculptor Gérard Choain.

The Champ de Mars, Admiral Bruat's fountain

Place des Six Montagnes Noires

THE PLACE DES SIX MONTAGNES NOIRES

This square owes its name to a hostelry, the most important in the Middle Ages, which stood on the site until 1880. The Roesselmann fountain, another work by Bartholdi, was installed there in 1882. In 1265 Jean Roesselmann, the town Provost, succeeded in retaking Colmar from the nobles and the supporters of the Bishop of Strasbourg, by whom he had been expelled, after re-entering it hidden in a barrel.

From the Place des Six Montagnes Noires two parallel streets lead to the Koïfhus. The Grand Rue, which until 1603 was called the Rue des Frères Mineurs, contains on both sides a lot of fine houses of which many are timbered, no. 84 being particularly picturesque with its two overhanging upper floors. The Rue Saint-Jean owes its name to the Order of St. John whose knights settled in Colmar during the first half of the 13th century. Of the church consecrated by Albert the Great in 1268 there remains only the choir, extensively rebuilt in the 19th century, and a trefoiled doorway supported by short columns and decorated on the corner stones with leaf heads. Another important building in this street is the one called the House of the Knights of St. John which was constructed in 1608 for a Colmar family by the architect Albrecht Schmidt. The lay-out of the building reminds one of that of an Italian palace.

LITTLE VENICE
THE KRUTENAU
THE QUAI DE LA
POISSONNERIE

The Krutenau is a district inhabited by market-gardeners to the
west of the Lauch river. Its main
street is the Rue Turenne. This
area is also called Little Venice
because of the waterway lined
with picturesque houses which
runs through it. Although it has
existed since 1209 it was originally
outside the fortifications of the
town and was only incorporated
into it in 1250. The bridge across
the Lauch was formerly the entrance to the town itself. It was also
called «the bridge by the watering
place» because of the large area
on its right where the market-gardeners watered their animals in
the river.
A very narrow little street, the Rue
de la Poissonnerie, lined with typical period houses, some of which
are in course of being restored,
leads to the Quai de la Poissonerie
whose name is a reminder of one
of the long established activities of
some of the citizens of Colmar.
The quay is lined with typical 16th
and 17th century houses whose
ground floors are in stone while
the upper stories are timbered.
Some of these houses were rebuilt
after the great fire of 1706. Parts
of the old town fortifications are
still visible on the other side of the
quay.

Little Venice

Grand Rue

Rue Saint-Jean

The Quai de la Poissonnerie

Rue du Chasseur   *Petite Rue des Tanneurs*

THE TANNERS' DISTRICT

This district is another reminder of a particular economic activity since up until the 18th century it was, in fact, entirely reserved for tanners. It has been restored thanks to the efforts of the Caisse Nationale des Monuments Historiques and of the Town of Col-mar. The houses, sited for the most part along the waterway, are absolutely typical. Very narrow and very tall, and built without basements, they rest on a high stone wall the upper stories having half-timbered cob-walls made from a mixture of straw and clay. The roofs are very extensive often having openings at several different levels, some set back relative to the others, thus permitting the tanners to dry their skins.

For the most part the houses date from the 16th, 17th and 18th centuries but the district itself is very much older. In fact the Rue des Tanneurs was enlarged in the 14th century and then again in 1883. Up until the French Revolution, beside the waterway, the mill canal or 'tanners' ditch' as it was called, there used to stand a tower, the Tanners' or Witches' Tower, against which stood a chapel, St. Michael's Chapel, mentioned in the 12th century, and a part of the original town wall.

THE OLD FRANCISCAN CHURCH

The Franciscan Order settled in Colmar in the middle of the 13th century. The church was built in large part in the 14th century but has been completely disfigured by subsequent transformations. The ceiling of the nave was lowered in the 14th century and a separating wall was built between the nave and the choir in the 18th century. Despite these modifications the Franciscan church remains a remarkable example of the architecture of the Mendicant Orders in Alsace.

In 1541 the Franciscans left Colmar. With the arrival of the Reformation in Colmar the church became a place of worship for the Protestants. A stained-glass window put up in 1926 commemorates the first Protestant service held in Colmar on 15th May 1575.

THE LITTLE WINE-GROWER

The present covered market was constructed in 1867 right beside the river Lauch thus allowing the market-gardeners to bring their fruit and vegetables to the market in large flat bottomed barges. Doors giving directly onto the waterway facilitate the unloading of the produce.

In the south west corner of the building, there is a niche, flanked by fluted columns supporting a richly decorated entablature, which contains a bronze statue by Bartholdi dated 1869. This is the little wine-grower. He is seated on a tree stump, accompanied by his dog, and tossing down his drink at a single draught.

Grand Rue, the Franciscan church

The Little Wine-Grower's fountain

Restored houses

THE RUE DES AUGUSTINS

The Augustines came to Colmar in 1316. The 14th century church and the monastery buildings were converted into a prison at the time of the French Revolution and finally demolished in the 19th century.

A detention centre was built on the site.

On the same side of the street, in the north façade of the Old Palace of the Sovereign Council, there is a fountain standing in a semi-dome niche with on top of it a bronze copy of the Mannecken-Pis presented by the city of Bruxelles in 1922.

On the other side of the street two houses attract attention. No. 6 has a beautiful Renaissance façade dating from 1599. No. 8 is the massive town residence of the Counts of Ribeaupierre who owned property in Colmar from the 13th century onwards. The most interesting part of this building is without a doubt the oriel on the corner.

Fountain in Rue des Augustins

Statue of Auguste Barthold

The Court of Appeal

THE STATUE OF AUGUSTE BARTHOLDI

This statue was executed by another Colmar sculptor, Louis Noël. Auguste Bartholdi was born in Colmar on 2nd August 1834. At a very young age he felt himself attracted to monumental statuary. From 1853 he exhibited at the Salon Officiel in Paris but his career was really launched by the statue of General Rapp following which he became the recognised sculptor of the town of Colmar. His fame rapidly spread beyond the bounds of his native town. He died on 3rd October 1904.

A large number of his projects and models are on exhibition in the Bartholdi Museum which has recently been reorganised.

THE COURT OF APPEAL

To the south of the Place Rapp there is a residential district of detached villas with gardens. It is also in this district that most of the administrative buildings of Colmar were constructed at the end of the 19th and the beginning of the 20th century: the Préfecture around 1860, the Hôtel des Postes (Central Post Office) in 1893, the Railway Station in 1905. It is a fact that during the period of German Administration, 1870-1918, the population of Colmar practically doubled going from 20,000 inhabitants in 1870 to more than 46,000 in 1913.

The most important buildings put up in this period are the Railway Station and the Court of Appeal.

The Station which, as shown by an inscription, was built in 1905-1906 is a vast brick construction whose shape, rather like that of a locomotive, also suggests in some of the elements of its decoration the architecture of fortifications.

Nearby, situated in a huge garden, is the massive building of the Court of Appeal. Constructed in 1906 in Neo-Baroque style it is distinguished by a mass of decorative elements (embossments, etc.) integrated into an overall pattern which focuses attention on the central building in the foreground with two smaller buildings sticking out from the main body in the wings. Next to the Court of Appeal, but set back a little, is the Waterworks, constructed at the same time as the water mains in the town, a large tower in the style of the fortified towers of the Middle Ages.

THE ROUTE DU VIN

The foothills of the Vosges halfway between the plain and the high barrier of the Vosges themselves, constitute a well defined region between two hundred and four hundred metres above sea level. The climate is relatively dry and sunny and the importance which wine-growing has attained here over the last two thousand years justifies the name of Route du Vin which is given to the greater part of this line of hills. Especially from Thann and Guebwiller to Obernai, the holdings, overlooked by the silhouettes of numerous ruined castles half hidden by the nearby forest, vary as much as the soils which are the outcome of a long and complex geological history. The villages and towns, often fortified, which line the route are evidence of the wealth provided by wine-growing and wine-making.

One has to leave Colmar, the traditional capital of the vineyards, and follow the Route du Vin from village to village to fully comprehend the way in which production is rooted in the individual holdings. The multiplicity of the terrains is one of the justifications for the planting of different types of grape in the vineyards of this zone of «Appellation d'origine contrôlée». Riesling, the best known of all, Tokay, Gewurztraminer, Muscat, red and white Pinots

and Sylvaner are the most important of these very characteristic vines. Their individual qualities make it possible to use these wines, and these alone, as the accompaniment to a fine meal from the aperitif to the dessert.

Techniques have evolved and the old wine-presses and huge wooden barrels have given way in many cases to modern installations. However if the Alsatian wine-growers have constantly improved their methods it has been in order to advance the art of wine-making. More than ever a walk across these meticulously maintained hills and a visit to their cellars provide ample proof of the love and care with which these great wines are produced. Although the costumes and other features of the folklore in evidence at the Wine Festivals in many villages show a marked loss in the cultural patrimony, once so rich and varied, the quality of the architectural features in most of these places, of which the following pages offer but a few examples, bear witness both to the antiquity and the vitality of this tradition of wine and vine.

The Alsatian vineyards

GUEBWILLER

Guebwiller, one of the more southerly of the small towns along the Route du Vin in Alsace, is on a spot which has many things in its favour. The town is situated on the right bank of the river Lauch near the spot where the Lauch valley runs into the Plain of Alsace. The name «Florival» which is given to this valley in itself suggests the nature of the landscape one finds there. One should not fail to visit the Romanesque churches at Murbach and Lautenbach in the Lauch valley.

Guebwiller has taken advantage of its situation and has based its development on various resources: the vineyards, of course, but industry also plays a very important role. From its Medieval past there remain several essential features.

St. Léger church, constructed at the end of the 12th and the beginning of the 13th centuries, shows the persistence in Alsatian architecture of Romanesque forms even in cases where certain Gothic techniques, such as the pointed vault, are used. To each of the vaults over the square bays of the central nave there correspond two bays in the aisles, and to this alternation of the supports is added a towering interior elevation; there is a large expanse of bare wall above the huge arcades, the high windows opening only a small part of the wall. Similarly the conception of the capitals and the doorway is close to that of 12th century Alsatian churches. Comparison with the apse which was reconstructed in the 14th century emphasizes the differences even more.

The Dominican Monastery which was built at the beginning of the 14th century adopts many features of the architecture of the Mendicant Orders in Alsace but in an original way, as is shown in particular by its wide rood screen.

The church of Our Lady which is connected with the transfer of the Benedictine Community from the abbey at Murbach in 1759, is an important example of 18th century religious architecture. The building was started by Beuque and then continued by G.I. Ritter after 1768. It has a majestic interior elevation in which tall Corinthian columns separate the nave from the aisles. Although only the south tower was ever completed and that somewhat belatedly, the pink limestone façade deserves to occupy a position of distinction in French Classical Art.

Guebwiller, the interior of the church of Our Lady

Guebwiller, church of St. Léger

On the previous pages:
typical Alsatian folkloristic costumes.

Rouffach, the Church of Notre-Dame.

Rouffach, the interior of the Church of Notre-Dame.

Obermorrschwihr, the Fountain with the Virgin.

EGUISHEIM

The wine-growing market town of Eguisheim owes its reputation to the exceptional quality of its rows of old houses which are remarkably well preserved, as well as to the wines produced by the vineyards which surround it. One can walk round this small town by following the old ramparts which like the houses are built around the castle in the centre.

The church of St. Peter and St. Paul is apt to be overlooked. Despite its modern reconstruction it has retained a Gothic bell-tower and above all an important example of Alsatian Romanesque sculpture — the doorway, executed in the first half of the 13th century. The tympanum shows Christ with his right hand raised in blessing, flanked by the apostles Peter and Paul, while on the left lintel the five Wise Virgins with their lamps advance straight towards the open door where Christ is waiting for them and on the right lintel the five Foolish Virgins stand in front of the closed door with their upturned lamps in their hands.

The silhouettes of the three castles of Eguisheim overlook the village and vineyard of Husseren from the first forest-covered slopes of the hill. The castle of Haut-Eguisheim is the oldest fort in Alsace according to the documentary evidence, since it is mentioned as early as the 11th century. The surviving building, together with those of the neighbouring Pflixbourg and Haut-Landsberg castles, dates essentially from the 12th and 13th centuries.

Eguisheim, the Rue du Rempart

Eguisheim, a panoramic view of the ruins of the "Three castles".

TURCKHEIM

Turckheim, a small wine-producing town near Colmar on the left bank of the river Fecht at the foot of the Brand hills, still has its city wall with its three gates as well as numerous old buildings. Although a member of the Decapole as early as 1354, it is from conflicts in the modern period that the town has suffered particularly. The name of Turenne remains associated with a battle won by that great strategist in 1675 in front of the city walls. The reconstruction of St. Anne's church in the 19th century spared the clock tower and square porch, the lower parts of which date from the 12th century while the upper parts are in the Gothic style.

Turckheim, the Porte de France

Sigolsheim, a view of the ancient village.

Katzenthal, a view of the village surrounded by vineyards.

KAYSERSBERG

Kaysersberg, situated where the valley of the river Weiss emerges into the Plain of Alsace, has a longer history than that of the castle which overlooks its vineyards and its Medieval buildings. «Caesaris Mons», «The Emperor's Hill», is mentioned in the Roman period. The village and the castle were acquired by the Emperor in the 13th century and fortified, becoming a free and imperial town which in the 14th century joined the Decapole.

The castle still has its 12th century keep with a commanding view over the town and the Weiss valley. The parish church was constructed over a long period from the 12th to the 16th centuries. Over the doorway the tympanum carved round about 1230-1235 is an example of Alsatian Romanesque art. It shows the Coronation of the Virgin flanked by the archangels Michael and Gabriel as is specified by the inscription, while the small figure one sees in the left hand corner is Conradus the master mason or sculptor of the doorway. The church furniture is very rich, but in the choir particular attention should be paid to the altar-piece by the sculptor Hans Bongart of Colmar which is dated 1518. Wooden bas-reliefs describing the Passion surround a Crucifixion while the predella shows Christ and the Apostles.

Kaysersberg, the castle

Kaysersberg, typical house, 90 Rue du Général de Gaulle

Kaysersberg, church showing Hans Bongart's altar-piece

RIQUEWIHR

Riquewihr is a small town situated in the very heart of the Alsatian wine-growing area. The village was mentioned for the first time in documents dated 1049 under the name «Richovilare». In the 11th century it was part of the property of the Counts of Eguisheim before passing in the 12th century into the hands of the Counts of Horbourg who fortified it in 1291 and conferred the status of town on it in 1320. In 1324 the town was sold to the Counts of Wurtemberg while in 1397 it was joined to the county of Montbéliard following the marriage of Henriette de Montfaucon with Eberhard de Wurtemberg. The Counts of Wurtemberg retained the lordship of the estate until the Revolution. At the end of the 15th century a Council, under the supervision of the Bailiff, the Count's representative, governed the town. In 1534 the Reformation was introduced in Riquewihr on the initiative of Count George of Wurtemberg Montbéliard.

Thanks to the vineyards and the wine trade Riquewihr enjoyed a period of great prosperity. In 1520 the Guild of Wine-growers was created whose offices today are at no. 42 Rue du Général de Gaulle. It was also in this period, about 1500, that the construction of a second city wall surrounded by a wide moat was undertaken. Certain features dating from the 13th century were incorporated into the new fortifications and altered appropriately, for example, the Thieves' Tower which owes its name to its function as a prison, and the Dolder. This high tower, which also served as a belfry, lost its role as the gateway to the town when the Porte Supérieure, furnished with a portcullis and a drawbridge, was constructed. The town's lower gateway was demolished in the 19th century. The town is laid out on either side of the main street within a quadrilateral. Of the medieval churches there remains almost nothing. The 12th century parish church was abandoned after numerous rebuildings. The church of Our Lady built in the Gothic style, was transformed into a Protestant presbytery at the time of the Reformation. St. Ehrard's church was similarly turned into a house after being

completely rebuilt.

The original castle was also demolished in order to replace it with a residence more to the taste of the period. Count George of Wurtemberg and his wife liked staying there and it even became his wife's principal residence after his death. It was finished in 1540 and was surrounded with auxiliary buildings a chancellery, stables, etc. After the Revolution it was turned into a school.

The magnificently sumptuous houses which line the streets and alleys date from the same period. It is impossible to mention them all since almost all the dwellings in Riquewihr go back to the 16th or 17th centuries and some are even older dating from the 15th century. Two houses are absolutely typical: the house known as Jung-Selig, no. 12-14 Rue du Général de Gaulle, and the house known as Dissler at 6 Rue de la Couronne. Jung-Selig which dates from 1561 is noteworthy for its high and wide half-timbered façade. Dissler, built in 1610 by Peter Burger, a member of the Town Council, illustrates the taste and wealth of the bourgeoisie of this period. This house has recently been the object of restoration by the Caisse Nationale des Monuments Historiques.

However the Thirty Years' War stopped development in this small town. In 1635 Riquewihr was beseiged and then pillaged by the troops of the Duke of Lorraine. After the Treaty of Westphalia in 1648 the town remained under the lordship of the Count of Wurtemberg Montbéliard even though it was under the sovereignty of the King of France. This situation persisted up until the Revolution. Indeed it was not until 1796 that Riquewihr became a French town.

The town underwent some modification during the 19th century, the churches and the Town Hall being rebuilt. The reputation of this little town continues to grow thanks to the quality and renown of its wines but also thanks to the picturesque nature of its old streets and dwellings which make it one of the most frequently visited tourist centres in Alsace.

Riquewihr, a view of the village.

Riquewihr the Porte Supérieure

Riquewihr the Dolder

Riquewihr, Jung-Selig House, 12-14 Rue du Général de Gaulle

HUNAWIHR

The most famous touristic resorts in Alsace, Riquewihr and Rebeauville, are considered to be among the most enchanting villages of the whole France. Hunawihr is known for its beautiful flower landscapes, for its wines, for its welcoming atmosphere and for the fortified church.
The city walls with their semicircular ramparts are an interesting example of military architecture. The tower lives on two different economic resources: vine-growing and tourism which benefits from the town's specific resources: the church, the stork restoration park the live exotic butterfly glass-house and the permanent orchid exhibition.

Hunawihr, a view of the village.

Colorful Hunawihr.

THE LIVE EXOTIC BUTTERFLY CENTRE

We are glad to offer you a splendid collection of exotic butterflies which live, free, in a luxuriant flora: a collection of orchids and of passion flowers.
Strolling through the botanical park or through the green-houses, the visitor discovers the fascinating and defenceless life of butterflies, following their entire life cycle from their birth.

THE ALSATIAN STORK RECOVERY CENTRE

The Centre now houses about 200 storks. Its aim is to have storks return to the Alsatian villages. Since 1976, from 30 to 50 couples reproduce in our park and in most of Alsatian and German villages. They represent about 80% of the total amount of storks present in the whole region.
Projects have aimed at organizing, in the best possible way, the natural environment destined to these birds so that they can live in total freedom. Since 1981 a show with the fishing animals is held regularly every afternoon.
A large aquarium was opened in 1983. It was made to house several cold water aquariums thus enabling the visitor to see over 20 species of fish which are original of the region.

A typical exotic butterfly from the Butterfly Glass-House.

Storks and a seal at the Stork Recovery Centre.

*Ribeauvillé: the Butchers' Tower
(Tour des Bouchers).*

RIBEAUVILLE

At the foot of the famous castles of Girsberg, Saint-Ulrich and Haut-Ribeaupierre, Ribeauvillé has preserved the charm of by-gone days. It still celebrates "Pfifferdag", the day of the wandering fiddlers who, in times gone by, used to pay homage to the lord of Ribeaupierre on the first Sunday in September.

The Grand'Rue is lined with old houses and the squares have fountains, such as the one in front of the 18th century Town Hall. Built in 1536 it is decorated with a lion bearing the arms of William I of Ribeaupierre.

The 13th century Tour des Bouchers or Butchers' Tower separates the upper town from the lower town. It was renovated and made higher in the 16th century.

KINTZHEIM

Kintzheim castle in the Bas-Rhin not far from Sélestat (not to be confused with Kientzheim, a little town near Colmar) is linked to the history of the noble family of Rathsamhausen. In plan it is a large rectangular ensemble containing various buildings. The façades facing the plain contain numerous windows and the circular keep overlooks all. Birds of prey, used for giving spectacular demonstrations, are raised here, which shows the uses to which these medieval castles, often set in splendid natural sites, can be put.

Kintzheim, panorama.

Kintzheim, the castle

Haut-Koenigsbourg, aerial view

Haut-Koenigsbourg, one of the castle doors.

THE HAUT-KOENIGSBOURG

The castle of the Haut-Koenigsbourg is built on a rocky platform rising up more than 720 metres from the Plain of Alsace to the south west of Sélestat. In the 12th century two castles separated by a wide moat, each with a square keep, were built there. The succession to the lordship during the 13th and 14th centuries was much disputed being coveted in particular by the Dukes of Lorraine and the Bishops of Strasbourg. Lorraine only renounced its rights to the lordship in 1474.

Already in 1454 it was besieged by Count Palatin. In 1462 it was almost completely destroyed being, in fact, the headquarters of a band of brigands who ransomed noblemen and merchants. It remained a ruin until 1479 when it was rebuilt by the Counts of Thierstein and the ruins which have been restored, date largely from this period. From 1519 to 1533 the castle was entrusted to military governors, then it was pledged and passed into the hands of the Sickingen family but, inhabited only by a provost, it was practically allowed to run to ruin. In 1606

56

Haut-Koenigsbourg, a corner of the castle.

Haut-Koenigsbourg, Banqueting Room

Haut-Koenigsbourg, The Knights' Hall

Rodolphe of Bollwiller had the defences rebuilt. At his death it was in the hands of the Counts of Fugger.

In 1633 the castle was besieged by a party of Swedes and after a siege of several months Philippe de Lichtenau, the commander of the fortress, surrendered. The castle was burnt down. Louis XIV, having become by the Treaty of Westphalia the sovereign of the province of Alsace in 1648, took the castle from the Fuggers and gave it back to the Sickingen family. They sold it in 1770 to the President of the Sovereign Council of Alsace, a man called Boug who kept the ruins until 1865. In 1865 after many changes of ownership

it was finally bought by the town of Sélestat who gave it to Emperor William II at the time of an official visit in 1899.

William II wanted to revitalize the Haut-Koenigsbourg and decided, in spite of strong opposition, to rebuild the castle. The work was started in 1900 under the supervision of Bodo Ebhardt, an architect who had already restored a large number of fortresses in Germany. The bulk of the work was finished in 1908. It is important to stress that this was not the restoration of a medieval castle but a reconstruction based much more on the architect's and the emperor's conception of the Middle Ages than on archeological realities. The

machicoulis, the brattices and the massive square keep with its embossments suggest the Neo-Gothic style of the end of the 19th or beginning of the 20th century rather than medieval military architecture. The interior was also entirely refitted. The murals are the work of Leo Schnug. The furniture, wainscoating and panelling, the arms and armour, and the other elements of the décor are also very typical of the period both in the taste for the monumental and in the mixture of styles.

The castle of the Haut-Koenigsbourg which was returned to France in 1919 is now maintained by the Caisse Nationale des Monuments Historiques.

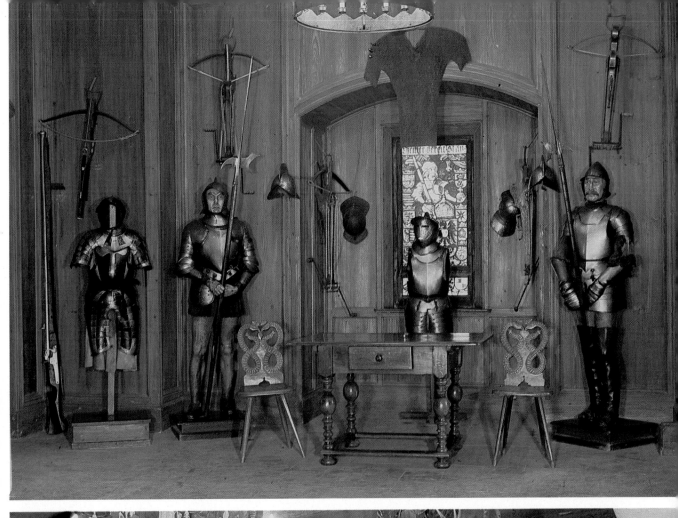

Andlau, a view of the castle.

Andlau, panorama.

Barr, a detail of the tower.

On the following pages:

Danbach, a typical example of the architecture of the village.

Blienschwiller, a typical Alsatian fountain.

Itterswiller, a typical life detail of the Alsatian towns.

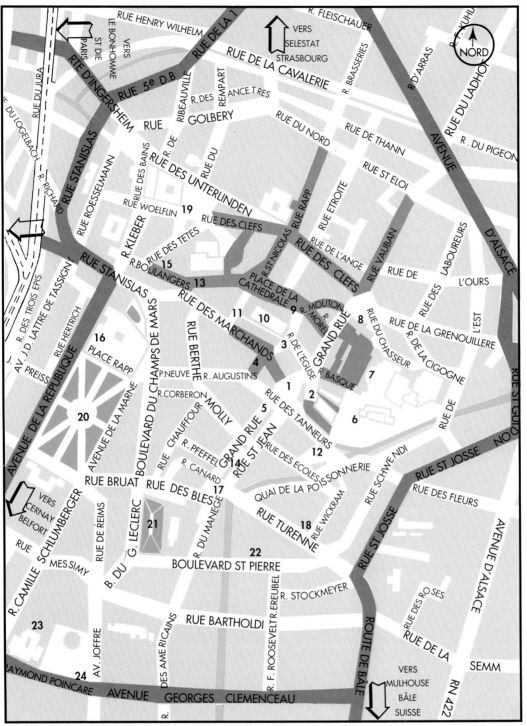

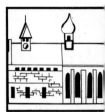

1- **Place de l'Ancienne Douane**
2- **Fontaine Schwendi**
3- **Maison Pfister**
4- **Musée Bartholdi**
5- **Palais de Justice**
6- **Quartier des Tanneurs**
7- **Ancien Hôpital**
8- **Ancienne Eglise des Franciscains**
9- **Collégiale Saint-Martin**
10- **Maison Adolph**
11- **Ancien Corp de Garde**
12- **Monument du vigneron alsacien**

13- **Eglise des Dominicains**
14- **Maison dite des chevaliers de St-Jean**
15- **Maison des Têtes**
16- **Place Rapp**
17- **Monument Roesselmann**
18- **Musée d'histoire naturelle**
19- **Musée d'Unterlinden**
20- **Monument de l'amiral Burat**
21- **Monument Hirn**
22- **La Petite Venise**
23- **Cour d'Appel**
24- **Statue d'Auguste Bartholdi**